ninety-nine

ninety-nine

THE HIGHER POWER

ALLAA AWAD

NINETY-NINE
THE HIGHER POWER

iUniverse books may be ordered through booksellers or by contacting:

iUniverse
1663 Liberty Drive
Bloomington, IN 47403
www.iuniverse.com
1-800-Authors (1-800-288-4677)

ISBN: 978-1-5320-4361-1 (sc)
ISBN: 978-1-5320-4360-4 (e)

Library of Congress Control Number: 2018902123

Print information available on the last page.

iUniverse rev. date: 03/15/2018

Dedicated to

The Realists

Introduction

At times, we open up and create dispositions of ourselves that we may be unfamiliar with. We find life so simple and glide effortlessly onward and upward. We never actually look at the base of what is guiding us. We overlook the true meaning of existence and how it is being directed.

However, there are the realists. The realists of miracle advocates. The entities who surrender to a greater power through no filtered lens beyond their capabilities. There is one, and only one, who we call forth by ninety-nine names. The real guide to finding what's in the heart and not in the brain is to trust and let go.

Through these odes of love and a Higher Power, you will find true allocations of God's attributes within you and this realm we live in. Understand it in the way you would normally. Your faith in the greater good will only denote the character you are. Read, reflect, and let it sink in.

1

Ar-Rahman

The All-Compassionate

Allaa Awad

I've been blessed
With you
But not by you.
But I've been blessed,
And it was composed for me
By someone who knows—
Someone we take for granted
Yet cascades us with blessings.

—*Thank you*

2

Ar-Rahim
The All-Merciful

Allaa Awad

I've repeated
And repeated
One hundred times more—
Salty cheeks become
Crystal.
I ask for forgiveness.
I tie my sins to you.
If my sins are frequent,
Then I won't have you,
Because you are better
Than me.
But he knows
What's in my heart.
And I'm only human.
I'm meant to sin, and he will forgive,
Whether it keeps me away from you
Or not.
I pick myself up once again.
Tomorrow is a new day.

—*Sinful*

3

Al-Malik

The Absolute Ruler

Allaa Awad

You think you know everything.
You think you know how I ought to feel
Or how I should act.
But you don't,
Because only that knows is the greater good,
Because he has guided my heart
To you.
Who can guide better than that?

—*He knows*

4

Al-Quddus
The Pure One

Allaa Awad

Purity comes within,
In the heart,
In the soul.
I have found it in you,
Just like God has perceived it to us.
It's clear as day
That your heart is unpolluted
And that you can love
And that you do love me.

—*Just let me in*

5

As-Salam

The Source of Peace

Allaa Awad

I'm at peace
With you.
I'm at peace
When I pray
For you
Or at least about you.
God hears me
In the midst of the night
As I kneel down and beg for you.
I have been promised that
I am being listened to.
Our names when merged
Mean only one thing,
Together, we are peaceful.

—*Salama*

6

Al-Mu'min
The Inspirer of Faith

Allaa Awad

Miracles
Are real, you know—
Valid.
I've witnessed several,
Like you,
Valid.
After I have asked for
Rain,
I meant something else,
But he has shown me
That he can give
But even better,
And it was you.
I have faith in him
To have faith in you.

—*You, you*

7

Al-Muhaymin
The Guardian

Allaa Awad

Thank you for
Watching over me
As I make the worst decisions
In this life—
This life that
We care so much about.
We seek justification within
Others,
Keeping you as a prominent thought
And how things can end,
Instead of thinking
Of meeting the only God
And how everything
Will end.

—*Protector*

8

Al-Aziz
The Victorious

Allaa Awad

We all desire victory,
Especially you.
We like to be better than others,
Especially you.
Or maybe not better than others,
But me, certainly.
You like to compete
Because it's in you.
Throw that away.
You'll never be as victorious
As the Victorious,
Ever.

—*Stay humble*

9

Al-Jabbar
The Compeller

Allaa Awad

It's 4:32 a.m.
I crave you,
But I don't call you.
I have no one to go to.
I then leave a puddle of tears
On the mat,
Forehead, nose down.
I get back up,
And I'm better
Because one call
To the heavens
Is the only call I need.

—*Your help, Ya Jabbar Ojborni*

10

Al-Mutakabbir

The Greatest

Respect
Is a rare attribute.
It is found in rare
Beings of the Higher Power.
We are guilty when we make
Ourselves higher than one another.
We are guilty for feeling supreme.
We must stay humble without
Pride,
For we are one and we shall
Return as one to the supremacy
Of this earth
To the one above
And beyond
The rights of everyone else.

—*Purity*

11

Al-Khaliq
The Creator

Allaa Awad

You call me beautiful
Like the moon,
Like sun,
Like the stars.
Thank you for resembling me
To the greatest creations
By the greatest Creator.
I am flattered.

—*Beautiful*

12

Al-Bari

The Maker of Order

Everything is designed
In complete chaos,
At least in our heads.
But little do you know
That this is the perfect order.
We are going the right way;
We are almost there.
Trust it.
Watch this.
You are mine.

—*Trust*

13

Al-Musawwir
The Shaper of Beauty

Allaa Awad

Everything is beautiful.
We are blind,
Very blind.
We see what we want.
We are negative.
Why are we so negative?
Open your eyes.
Discover a realm that
You think you can't imagine.
Once you imagine,
It has become real.
This is real.
I am real; you are real,
Together we are shaped into something
Beautiful.

—*You and I*

14

Al-Ghaffar
The Forgiving

Imagine…
Would your mother
Throw you in a pit of
Fire?
Would she tear
Your heart apart?
No, but people would—
Ungodly people
Would—
However, God won't.
I promise you
Because he promised me.

—*Forgiver | Mother & God*

15

Al-Qahhar
The Subduer

Allaa Awad

You've made my blood
Boil,
Like heated
Sunrays—
Or, even worse,
Your heart exploiting
Mine
Through my blood,
Underneath my skin,
Into my veins.
Just one prayer
To the Subduer
Is all it took
To give you a taste
Of your own
Medicine.

—*Relief*

16

Al-Wahhab
The Giver of All

Allaa Awad

Gifts
Should be sentimental.
However,
I ask for mine,
I ask for you,
And he responds
Because you are sentimental,
And you are mine.

—*Gift from God*

17

Ar-Razzaq
The Sustainer

Allaa Awad

I am rich.
I have a heart
Inside a rib cage.
Together, I am a masterpiece.
I have eyes; I can see you.
I can see your beauty.
I have a heart that loves you.
Can you see how rich I am?

—*Blessed*

18

Al-Fattah
The Opener

Allaa Awad

I am trying to find you.
To find what's in your heart
Is like trying to
Open a safe without its key.
Actually, you told me that,
And eventually you did.
For he is the opener of all doors,
The opener to good
Through guidance.
There may be closed doors,
But he has opened several,
And taking the risk to go in
Is the key.
Trust blindly,
And you will simply
Get there.

—*Blind faith*

19

Al-Alim
The Knower of All

What lies underneath my
Skin,
He only knows.
The solid truth,
Love,
Pure love.
You may not know—
Or act like
You don't—
But you do.
I know you do,
Just like he knows
You know.

—*Truth*

20

Al-Qabid

The Constrictor

Allaa Awad

Take away
Love;
Take away
Fear.
Only you can do that,
But please
Don't rip my heart out,
Even if it's bad for me.
Make it better for me.
I know you can
Because no one else can.

—*Painless*

21

Al-Basit

The Reliever

I cry with heartache.
I kneel
On the floor.
I can't get up.
Forehead down,
Nose glued,
Plead.
You've asked,
And so I did.
I get back up,
Relieved.
I do it again.

—*Assistance*

22

Al-Khafid

The Abaser

Allaa Awad

Ease love,
Ease pain,
But show me why.
Why he's
In my life
At this time.
Please don't do this
Anymore.
Reduce pain,
Reduce love.

—*This one*

23

Ar-Rafi
The Exalter

Allaa Awad

You raise me up,
Adrenaline running
Through my heart.
You raise me up.
You give me
What I deserve.
I deserve you.
I don't ask, "Why?"
I just know
Because he gives
What you perceive,
And you are the best.

—*I love you*

24

Al-Mu'izz

The Bestower of Honors

Allaa Awad

Unattainable—
At least that's what it seems.
Can I meet you for a second?
Are you there?
Can you hear me?
If so,
Blink once.
Through light
Or sound,
Just show me.
Though,
You've showed me
Through love
And mercy,
Through my beating heart
That carries anxiety until
I am his.

—*Understood*

25

Al-Mudhill

The Humiliator

Allaa Awad

Mistreated and
Misunderstood,
What proof do
You need?
This isn't enough?
Your beating heart
Over every breath—
What more do you want?
You've humiliated his
Existence.
You never believed in
Faith.
Why though?

—*Proof given*

26

As-Sami

The Hearer of All

Allaa Awad

Vibrations
Into the core of the
Earth,
I yearn for you,
God.
Please,
I have had enough.
Sending pleas
To your
Throne,
I know you are there.
I know you want this.
How much longer?
I know you're
Listening to
Me begging.
Is what you want to
Hear
Thank you?

—*Sounds*

27

Al-Basir

The Seer of All

Midnight,
12:22,
You are there for
Me.
You see me.
I can't see you.
You see my heart,
My tears.
I can't see you,
But you are
In my
Premises,
Next to me,
Side by side,
Helping me.

—*Not so blind*

28

Al-Hakam

The Judge

Allaa Awad

You think you're
Bad for me,
And I don't deserve
You
Because you are
Sinful.
But I love it
When you are
Sinful
And aware
Of your actions
Contradicting mine.
But who am I
To judge?
Who is anyone
To judge?

—*Critical*

29

Al-Adl

The Just

Allaa Awad

Chances:
You don't ever consider
A second one.
You've said
That we aren't perfect,
So please
Don't contradict
Your words.
Who are you?
God?
Well, I'll tell you.
God told you and I
That our chances
Will always be laid out on the table.

—*Infinite chances*

30

Al-Latif
The Subtle One

Allaa Awad

Broken hearts,
Or even worse,
Shattered
Souls.
But when I pray
For protection,
He will make sure
That my heart will
Never be broken,
And my soul will
Remain just.

—*Safeguarded*

31

Al-Khabir
The All-Aware

Allaa Awad

Your intentions
Are clean.
You say,
Your intentions are
Discreet,
But are they clean?
What are you scheming?
I may not know,
But he knows,
And I speak to him
Every night.

—*Unconcealed*

32

Al-Halim

The Clement One

Allaa Awad

Not only am I
Patient,
But you are too,
Through thick and thin,
For better or for worse.
I sin and sin
Consciously,
But you always
Forgive.
Thank you for your patience,
Therefore, I am patient
Too.

—*Moderate*

33

Al-Azim

The Magnificent

Allaa Awad

I call for you
Upon your greatest name
That is, till this day,
Unknown.
We are enlightened
With ninety-nine,
But there is one
Which I seek,
And I will know
When I meet you.

—*Greatest*

34

Al-Ghafur

The Forgiver and Hider of Faults

Allaa Awad

Thank you for
Keeping my sins
Safe.
But even better,
Overlooking them.
I may not have asked,
And I may not deserve it,
I might be humiliated
Within myself,
But you
Have forgiven
And kept me
Innocent.

—*Moved on*

35

Ash-Shakur

The Acknowledging One

Allaa Awad

Showered benedictions
From the greatest,
I don't deserve this.
I am greedy.
I am selfish.
But you manage
To make yourself
Blind deliberately
To these flaws.
All I ask
Is for this power.
I yearn to become
Blind, deliberately
And willingly,
To contradictions
Of these people
Who create demeanors of themselves
Of angelic attributes.
Keep me optimistic.
I pray for
Optimism.

—*Forever thank you*

36

Al-Ali
The Highest

Allaa Awad

Sky is the limit;
At least
That's what they say.
But little do you recall
That there is a sky.
And then there is
Divinity,
Beyond our imaginations.

—*Divine*

37

Al-Kabir
The Greatest

Allaa Awad

The supreme
Of most
Of all
Creations
Is greater than
Infinite skies,
Greater than
Beating hearts
Across the universe,
Shining stars
Across the galaxy,
A million years away.
But we are so close
To meeting the
Higher Power.
One blink of an eye,
And we are there.

—*Meet you*

38

Al-Hafiz

The Preserver

Allaa Awad

Being saved
Can mean two
Things:
To be saved
From the
Bad
Is called love;
To be saved for
Something
Is called
Patience.
And he only
Preserves
The best.

—*Wait for it*

39

Al-Muqit

The Sustaining One

Allaa Awad

I've felt
Cultivated by
God,
And I've felt
Cultivated
By you.
I just know that God
Has ordered your heart
And soul
To cultivate me,
Myself,
For he is the greatest
At nourishing.

—*Lead the way*

40

Al-Hasib

The Reckoning One

Allaa Awad

When we are negative,
Or when someone
Other than you
Is negative,
We take it into account
For everything.
Yet we never
Realize how much
The greater power
Is taking us into account
For the minor
Things we
Do.
So who are you?

—*Everything counts*

41

الجليل

Al-Jalil
The Mighty

Allaa Awad

I've lost you,
You've lost me,
But we'll make
Our way
Back to one another.
Together we are one
Diamond,
Lost at sea,
Buried in the grounds
Of this earth.
Yet we'll find our way
Because nothing is lost.
No matter how deep
We are dug
Or how small,
Nothing is too big
Or too small.
We will return
Like sea to shore.

—*Lost and then found*

42

Al-Karim
The Generous

Allaa Awad

I've fed the unfortunate,
And so have you.
I've given love,
And so have you.
You've given me
Your love.
How generous is that?
Living in this world of
Corruption,
You still give
Abundantly,
Even though I never
Asked for it.
You've given us
More than we
Deserve,
Yet we are still
Selfish.

—*Selfish*

43

Ar-Raqib
The Watchful One

Watching you
Religiously.
Don't get me
Wrong,
Not like that.
But I watch
How our hearts
Vibrate on the same frequency
Of existence.
God watches over me
As I watch our hearts
Collide.

—*Connected*

44

Al-Mujib

The Responder to Prayer

Allaa Awad

Prominent prayer?
You.
Prominent thought?
You.
I beg into the
Unknown, as you might say,
But I beg with confidence
Into thin air
Because he is listening,
And he will be the only one to
Respond.

—*No one else*

45

الواسع

Al-Wasi

The All-Comprehending

Allaa Awad

He's given us
Space,
Enough space
For trials and
Errors.
He's given us
Heartaches,
But only for
One reason—
To hear our
Voices.
And once he hears our
Voices,
He opens up
Opportunities
That we thought were
Unreachable.

—*Opened doors*

46

Al-Hakim

The Perfectly Wise

Allaa Awad

We think we can
Manipulate others
Without thinking
How wise
The Higher Power is.
Why act ungodly?
Does God manipulate
Us?
No.
God has ordered us to be
Righteous,
To be wise
Because once we make
Irrational decisions,
We become irrelevant
To him.

—*Kind hearts*

47

Al-Wadud

The Loving One

Allaa Awad

Our mothers love
Us
Unconditionally,
And he loves us
Seventy times more.
How does that feel?
I have no
Idea,
But I see my mother
Cry for me when she is
Happy.
I wonder what
God feels when he's happy for
Me?

—*Smile*

48

Al-Majid

The Majestic One

Spiritual slavery
Is what I like to
Call it.
Not your typical bow
Down,
But your gratitude and
Satisfaction
Are the only slavery acts
We need
To send out love
To the heavens of this earth.

—*Gratitude*

49

Al-Ba'ith
The Infuser of New Life

Allaa Awad

Months are turning into
Days.
Decades are turning into
Years.
Our souls will taste
Death.
We will be once again
Awakened
To the sounds of
Horns.
We will all meet
You
Surrendered or not.

—*Alive again*

50

Ash-Shahid
The Witness

Allaa Awad

Wake up in the morning
With a facade.
Begin your day
With a
Facade,
A facade of innocent
Whereabouts
To manipulate,
Yet you know exactly what's
In your heart.
Don't step over it.
Don't deny it.
I may not see,
And now you are in
Denial.
But we have one
Witness.

—*Enough*

51

Al-Haqq
The Truth

Allaa Awad

Big bang theories,
Homo sapiens,
Times,
One atom.
We go back
In intervals,
But where did this atom
Come from?
How was it
Conducted?
Are we imprudent
To this confusion
That is being dragged
When we have all the
Verifications—
From beating hearts
To taken souls,
To buried graves,
To newborn wombs?

—*Clear*

52

Al-Wakil

The Trustee

I trust you
Because I trust
Him.
I trust that he had
Gifted me
You
To learn how to trust
In him.
Everything happens for a purpose,
You know.
So I trust you
Because I trust him.
This isn't a coincidence;
There are *no* coincidences.
Trust this process.
Now trust me.

—*Trust me please*

53

Al-Qawiyy
The Possessor of All Strength

Allaa Awad

I was once asked,
"If God is so strong,
Can he create a rock
So heavy
That he himself
Cannot pick it up?"
I answered
With poise,
"Yes, if it's in his will to."

—*Competent*

54

Al-Matin
The Forceful One

Allaa Awad

You were 598 miles
Away from me.
I prayed.
You went even
Farther.
I prayed.
You were 4,150 miles
Away.
I prayed.
We parted
Five months.
You were then
1,205 miles
Away.
I prayed.
You are now
598 miles
Away.
I pray.

—*Square one*

55

Al-Waliyy
The Governer

Allaa Awad

We are ordered and
Organized
To follow a
Systematic ritual
That will lead
Us
To the center of
This spiritual act,
To our originator,
To our only
Creator.

—*Gut instincts*

56

Al-Hamid
The Praised One

Allaa Awad

7.6 billion
People,
And we praise
Your existence.
Now let's
Quadruple that;
Count the birds,
The ants,
The trees,
And everything
That has a
Heart,
Everything that
Breathes.
We will all come home
To you.

—*Honor the honorable*

57

Al-Muhsi
The Appraiser

Allaa Awad

We act like
We know
Everything.
We can feel, yes.
We can see, yes.
We are surrounded by
Auras.
Our thoughts are lingering
In between
Quantum fields,
So we claim that we know
Everything.
But you
Are the source of all knowings.
You are the reader of all
Reflections.
You know all our so-called
Secrets,
And yet you
Keep us safe with all your
Knowings.

—*Evaluate me*

58

Al-Mubdi
The Originator

Allaa Awad

Before life,
There was a realm
That cannot be explained
Nor interpreted.
We do not have knowledge
Of past existence.
We abide by the religions'
Guidelines
To become moral,
To become ethical.
You are the Creator of
Entities that exist
Today,
Created so perfect
Without any assistance
Or ramifications,
All designed in a flawless
Matter
And in seamless order.

—*Unique pieces*

59

Al-Mu'id

The Restorer

"You only live once"
Is a common saying
Among the individuals
Of this jurisdiction,
True.
We take for granted
The life that has been given to
Us.
We barely keep in mind that
We will live once again
For eternity.
We will come back to life
After death.
We will come back to life
By the power and demand of
You.
We shall see what life really
Meant.

—*See you*

60

Al-Muhyi

The Giver of Life

You have given us
Life
With no one else.
You have given us
A brain
To construct,
While you have given us
A heart
To do the thinking.
You have given us the
Power
To become one
With ourselves
For you.

—*Born*

61

Al-Mumit
The Taker of Life

There is a difference
In when to control
Your own life,
Make rational decisions
In everyday situations.
We have the power
And the mind
To know what is right
And what is immoral.
But we don't have the
Power and
Authorization
To take away
Something beautiful—
A blessing,
A sanction,
A chance.
All the above
Equals your life.

—*Endings*

62
٦٢

Al-Hayy
The Ever-Living One

We don't live
Forever.
We aren't responsive
To eternity,
Nor can we strive for it,
For everything is
Momentary.
We will experience
Ever living,
When our lives
Come to an end,
And we shall meet
The Higher Power,
The base of
Ever living.

—*Forever*

63

Al-Qayyum
The Self-Existing One

Allaa Awad

Seven billion people,
Seven billion souls,
Living,
Breathing,
Praising,
Or at least a great
Portion do implore
A realm that does not
Exist tangibly,
But mystically,
All created by
One
Who does not
Live,
Does not breathe,
Does not praise,
Cannot be seen
Nor touched
But can be felt
In the hearts of
The well connected
To the ever living
And the existence of
One.

—*One and prevailing*

64

الواجد

Al-Wajid

The Finder

Allaa Awad

I am in absolute need
Of something virtuous.
I have nothing
But you.
I am deprived,
But you are not.
You give prosperity.
You bequest contentment.
Impossible does not exist
In your word list.
Hence, I need you,
For you have everything.

—*Find it*

65

Al-Majid
The Glorious

We know what great is.
We are aware of
Magnificence.
We try to become
Glorious in this
World.
We strive for
Success and to become
Wealthy
Because this is all we
Know.
We are unaware
Of supremacy.
Our brains don't have
The capacity
To understand a higher
Power
Or to even understand
True magnificence.
We weren't designed to
For one reason:
Glory belongs to one—
God.

—*Praise*

66

Al-Wahid

The Unique, the Single

"He has created us
In pairs."
We all know,
We all have read,
We all have memorized.
Throw your ego out the
Window.
You need someone,
I need someone,
You need me,
And I need you
To complete this journey called
Life.
We need each other.
He, however,
Does not.
He is alone.
He is one.
He is unique.

—*Figure it out*

67

Al-Ahad
The One, the Indivisible

Allaa Awad

No one
But the One.

—*Single, not plural*

68

As-Samad
The Satisfier of All Needs

Allaa Awad

We rely on
Others
To complete our happiness.
We rely on others
For guidance,
For assistance.
We then get disappointed
When we choose the wrong ones.
At times we keep
Falling
For one reason;
To rely on who created you,
Who initially made you,
Who understands you more than
Your mother,
Your best friend,
Your sister,
Your brother.
Become reliant to
Him,
And he will never do you
Wrong.

—*Concede*

69

Al-Qadir
The All Powerful

Allaa Awad

You were my wish;
You still are.
You are what I want.
We encountered misunderstandings
Together.
You left.
All I could think of was
How do I get you to come back?
My mom didn't know.
But she did tell me
That nothing is impossible,
And there is only one person
Who can help.

—*One solution*

70

Al-Muqtadir
The Creator of All Power

Nothing is too immense
For you.
You show us that
Every day.
I have one simple request.
I know you are testing my
Patience,
And I am keeping my patience
Intact
Only because of you.
You have promised
That all prayers are
Answered
Only because you
Can.

—*Endless possibilities*

71

Al-Muqaddim
The Expediter

We have been told that
Everything has been already
Written
Prior to our
Existence.
We are set up by
The Higher Power
With what he
Wishes.
We are put in this dimension
To follow a
System,
But to follow the gut
Of our own selves.
He will impose
When necessary
What he wishes will
Befall.
And what he does not
Wish for will
Deteriorate.
We can change our
Destinies
With one simple act:
Prayer.

—*Think ahead*

72

Al-Mu'akhkhir
The Delayer

Allaa Awad

We pray and
Beg.
We do what you have
Asked.
Prominent prayers
Become our prominent
Thoughts.
I will continue to request
What I've been longing for
Because you want to me to,
You have guided me to.
Even if it takes years,
I know that eventually I will get
There
Because the way I perceive you
Is that I know you will give me
What I intend for
Because you have
Promised.
And you don't break
Promises.

—*Time and more time*

73

Al-Awwal
The First

Proper divine intelligence
Is only known by you.
We tend to overthink and use our brains
That eventually becomes a devilish
Thought.
"Who created God?"
Is an ongoing question.
No one created God.
He is the very first;
It's as simple as that.
It's like asking
Why can't men give
Birth?
There is no valid answer.
It's just the way it is.

—*First and foremost*

74

Al-Akhir

The Last

Our lives will
End
Eventually.
We cannot
Hide or run
From death.
It is inevitable to become
Immortal.
Immortality does not exist.
But the only One who will stay
Alive
Is our Creator, our center.
Even after the end,
One existence will remain
The same.

—*Ultimate*

75

Az-Zahir

The Manifest One

Allaa Awad

When we question
The Higher Power,
We question with dumbfounded
Causes.
We don't need proof
Of physical existence.
Sometimes there is such thing
As an
Imprudent question.

—*Less thinking*

76

Al-Batin
The Hidden One

Vibes and auras
Are beautiful
Aspects of an
Individual.
We are created
With these traits
To understand
And connect with
Each other.
This is enough to suffice.
Gut feelings
And being true to your
Heart
Are enough to suffice
The power of the
Higher Power.

—*Inner you*

77

Al-Wali

The Protector

Allaa Awad

We are our own guides,
Yet we have a leader.
We own things,
But we don't own our minds
Or our hearts,
As said and told.
I don't love you
For no reason.
I have been channeled
To the same frequency
As yours.
My heart has been guided
And led
To love you.

—*Safeguarded*

78

Al-Muta'ali
The Supreme One

Allaa Awad

Nothing can be compared
To you.
Not a synonym
Nor an acronym,
No derivative,
No imitation,
Nothing above you,
Nothing below you.
But that doesn't mean
That we can't reach
You,
So high up
Yet right next to
Us.

—*Closer than you think*

79

Al-Barr
The Doer of Good

We meet people
For a reason.
At times,
We are meant to meet
Someone for guidance
Or simply become the
Guide.
We are meant to
Benefit one another
Spiritually, physically.
Again, no coincidences.
This dynamic system of
Life exists to show us
That he is the doer of good,
And we are led to lead
One another.
I have led you,
And you have led
Me.

—*I am good*

80

Al-Tawwab

The Guide to Repentance

Allaa Awad

We sin and look
At it as a bad thing.
But have you ever
Questioned
That maybe we are meant to
Sin
So that we could get closer to
Him?
So that at least he gets to hear our
Voices
Speak to him,
And that we acknowledge his
Existence?
We aren't unflawed,
And we aren't ideal.
But we sin because
He will forgive us.
All we need to do is
Repent and recognize.

—*Endless chances*

81

Al-Muntaqim
The Avenger

Allaa Awad

We judge and
Punish
With our observances
And whereabouts.
We seize one another
With heartless actions
When really there is only
One
Who can judge
Anything and anyone.
Keep your intentions
Clean, and you shall
Rise.

—*Unpretentious*

82

Al-`Afuww
The Forgiver

Allaa Awad

We don't talk about our
Sins,
Like it's taboo.
It is in a way,
And we can't disclose
What we have committed
Because we are humiliated
And ashamed.
But open your eyes,
And be aware of how you feel.
If that is how you feel,
You are the going the right
Way.

—*Guilty and aware*

83

Ar-Rauf

The Kind One

Allaa Awad

We are created with
Love
And to be loved.
We are not created to sin
And go to hell.
We are created to understand
Morality and real depictions
Of life.
He has mercy on our souls
Once we just comprehend
The Higher Power,
The mercifulness of all falls upon
our souls.

—*Grace*

84

Malik-Al-Mulk
The Owner of All

Allaa Awad

This kingdom or
Universe, as we like to call our
Home,
Is created with dominance and
Allegiance
In seven days.
Perfectly constructed
To fit 7.6 billion
Entities of worth,
All living to strive
One goal:
Self-importance.
We do not own this
Kingdom or universe.
So why be a
Narcissist?
We are not any dominant to
Each other.
We are one entity of
The Higher Power.

—*The kingdom we live in*

85

Zul-Jalaali-wal-Ikram
The Possessor of Majesty and Honor

Allaa Awad

He wants what
We want.
Nothing more,
Nothing less.
We are driven to pray
For one reason.
He wants to grant
What we desire.
He wants to cherish
And transmit gratitude
Into our hearts.
Generosity is an
Understatement
Of what he is.
You once told me,
In our distant days,
That you will see me
Soon
And that no matter what we're told
If God says Kun Fayakun.
So until then,
I will
Be persistent
And stable,
Wishing for it,
Asking for it;

—*Kun fayakun, "Be, and it is"*

86

Al-Muqsit
The Equitable One

As humans,
We are able to articulate
Two feelings:
Positivity and negativity.
We have the curiosity voyage
To compel one of these to our everyday
Thoughts,
And that is
Negativity.
When thoughts become
Things,
We tend to
Blame the universe for
Manifesting such outcomes.
The Higher Power is the
Fairest.
You make your destiny
By simply attracting what you
Want.

—*Justifiable*

87

Al-Jami'
The Gatherer

We've been told that our
Souls
Have met
In a time that we do not
Recall.
It makes perfect
Sense.
The logic was proven
When I met
You.
Immediate connection in a
Time span of
Two days
Was all it needed
For it to
Flourish
Into something
Exceptional.
We were perfectly
Joined by the
Only One who has the power
To collect
And merge one another.
He knows best
Of who is meant to
Encounter and
Love one another.

—*Connection of hearts*

88

Al-Ghani

The Rich One

Allaa Awad

We need him;
He doesn't need us.
We are poor without
Him.
We praise and believe,
Not for him,
But for us.
For inner peace,
For recognizing,
For inner wealth.
And the only thing
That can fill up our
Needs
Is him.

—*Wealth within*

89

Al-Mughni

The Enricher

Allaa Awad

I am unfortunate
Without you.
My actions do not suffice on
My own.
I seek for guidance
And assistance
To reach to you.
Not to my mother,
But to who really knows me,
To someone who can fulfill
My wants and needs.
I am not afraid to ask for what I
Want
Because I deserve it
From you.

—*Rich by you*

90

Al-Mani'

The Preventer of Harm

Allaa Awad

What we desire
May not be worthy
For us.
We are not entitled
To let it
Go.
We are entitled
To embrace what we
Might think is good
For us.
And once it is
Gone,
We only then can
See
The power of his
Safety
Being applied to us,
The love he has
To teach you a
Lesson
Because, keep in
Mind,
That he only tests
His loved ones.

—*Purpose*

91

Ad-Darr

The Creator of the Harmful

Allaa Awad

We are all aware
That life is all about
Assessments
Of adversity
And privileges.
But for some,
Adversity is
Hidden
For a period of
Time.
That only when you
Decide to open your
Eyes,
That it is has been there,
Whether in the gut
Or the brain.
You suggested to
Overlook it.
Nevertheless, it has been there
All along.

—*Endure*

92

An-Nafi

The Creator of Good

Allaa Awad

I pray almost
Anywhere,
Anytime,
Anyplace.
Sometimes even
Involuntarily.
People look at me
And wonder,
Did that person say something?
Little do they know
That prayers are countered
Anywhere,
Anytime,
Anyplace.
The benefits
Of the Higher Power
Are accessible,
Even while stuck in
Traffic.
Envision the outcomes
Of your prayers,
And let the emotion
Exist.
All it takes is one simple
Feeling:
Belief.

—*Wishes*

93

An-Nur
The Light

Allaa Awad

Our minds cannot
Comprehend your
Looks
Or your features.
All we know are your
Attributes.
Within these names of
Sacred elements,
We call upon you,
And we can only feel you.
We become enlightened
Because you are light,
The light within us.

—*Enlighten my heart*

94

Al-Hadi
The Guide

Allaa Awad

You told me not think with my
Brain.
You told me that my heart is
Weak,
But someone else told me
The opposite.
It is even proven in manuscripts
And miracles,
That we hold and recite.
Every day,
I have been guided to you
Because my heart is not attached,
But conscious
Of what he is telling me.
And that is
To continue to pray
For you.

—*Heart, not brain*

95

Al-Badi

The Originator

Allaa Awad

I am not like you.
Nor are you like me.
We may have similar
Traits,
But I am unique,
And so are you.
And so is your
Mother.
And so is your
Father.
We might take a few
Characteristics,
But we are one,
And we have never been in
Existence in this dimension
Before.
We are incomparable
By the Creator of perfect
Souls.
We are not copied.
Nor are we duplicated.
We are seamlessly designed
In complete innovation.

—*Originality*

96

Al-Baqi

The Everlasting One

Allaa Awad

Live forever?
Not in this dimension.
Death might seem
Too far drawn to
Envision.
We will taste it,
Whether we can
Conceive it or
Not.
We will surrender
Forcefully,
Except for
The ever living.

—*Raw truth*

97

Al-Warith

The Inheritor of All

Allaa Awad

We live for a purpose.
We exist for One.
We are owned
By our guardians.
We are owned by our
Souls.
Our souls are fragile
Yet strong with devotion.
We will eventually return
To the origins of our souls,
And that is him.
We shall return to him,
To the inheritor of this earth,
To the inheritor of all creations.
There shall be nothing left on this
Domain.
Eventually it will become
Nothing.

—*Back to you*

98

Ar-Rashid

The Righteous Teacher

Allaa Awad

We make irrational
Decisions,
Like I made before
You.
I was lost
And needed pure guidance.
I prayed for rain
In order to communicate with
Him.
I got my answer.
He has guided me
And will not mislead me.
You've told me
That I've opened a window
For you,
But that wasn't me.
It was God leading you to
Me.
I'll explain to you
One day.
Just let me back in.

—*The idea of a second chance*

99

As-Sabur

The Patient One

Allaa Awad

We are full of
Flaws.
We are full of
Anger.
We are full of
Mistakes.
We are versatile
To any encounters
Of good or bad.
We are influenced by
Others,
Good or bad.
We take time to
Find ourselves.
We have been tested,
And at times we fail.
We seek refuge from ourselves.
We then discover that it is not ourselves
That can help us.
We know nothing,
And we may never know,
But somehow
And somewhere
We find peace in our hearts to go back to you.
You are patient.
You are kind enough to not take our
Flaws, anger, and mistakes to account.
Endless chances are given.
I just shed a tear.
You give us what we don't think we deserve,
But you are the Generous,
And you are the Loving One.

You are the Preserver, and you are
The Sustainer.
We learn tolerance from you.
You diffuse patience into our hearts.
You are with us at all times.
As said, there are no derivatives of
You.
But we try to become at least
Good, like you,
To please you,
And I pray that one day
We will meet you,
To meet the All-Compassionate,
Despite our flaws and mistakes,
Because you are
The Patient One.

—*Patience*

EPILOGUE

To conclude such spiritual content, everything is explained and perceived in your own way of beliefs and principals. In my perception of The Higher Power or what I like to call him, God, is something that I hold with high regard. If you know me, I connect every encounter in life to the greater good. Everything is aligned in perfect order, whether it be good or bad. While writing these odes of faith; countless thoughts were scrutinized to its' essence. These protruding reflections were triggered by people. People whom I have affected and inspired and of course who has impacted me through storms and tranquility.

I trust this book will end up in safe hands.

Printed in the United States
By Bookmasters